ANIMAL FARM: FUN FACTS ABOUT FARM ANIMALS

SPEEDY
PUBLISHING

Speedy Publishing LLC
40 E. Main St. #1156
Newark, DE 19711
www.speedypublishing.com

Farm animals are bred
for many purposes.

Pigs are very smart animals. A pig's snout is an important tool for finding food in the ground and sensing the world around them. On many farms, pigs are kept indoors in sheds with cement floors, and some are caged.

Cows are herbivores meaning they eat grasses and plants. They eat 50 pounds of food a day. Cows produce most of the milk that people drink. A cow can produce 6 gallons of milk a day

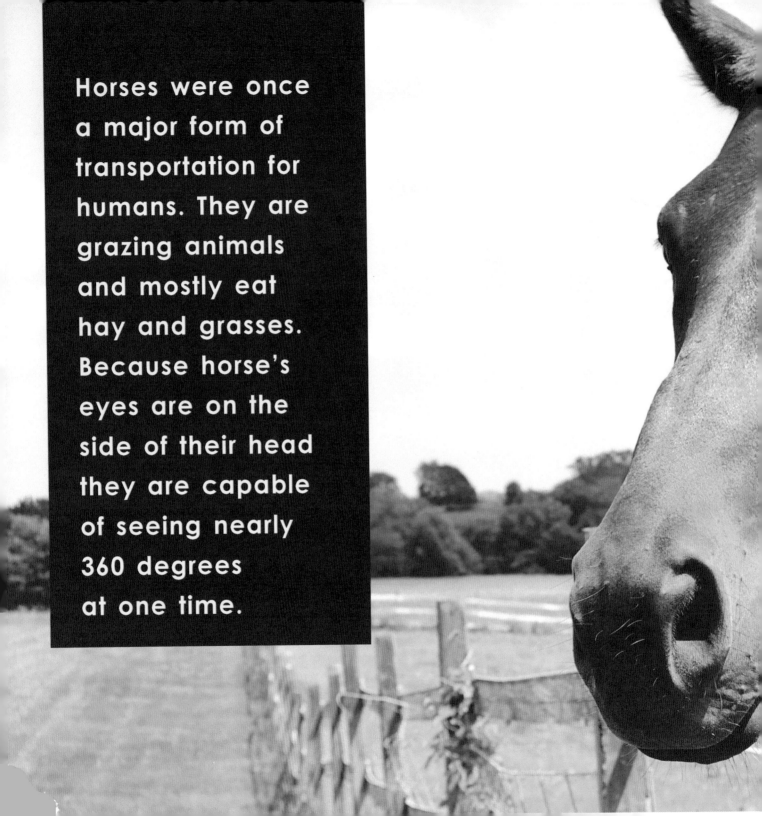

Horses were once a major form of transportation for humans. They are grazing animals and mostly eat hay and grasses. Because horse's eyes are on the side of their head they are capable of seeing nearly 360 degrees at one time.

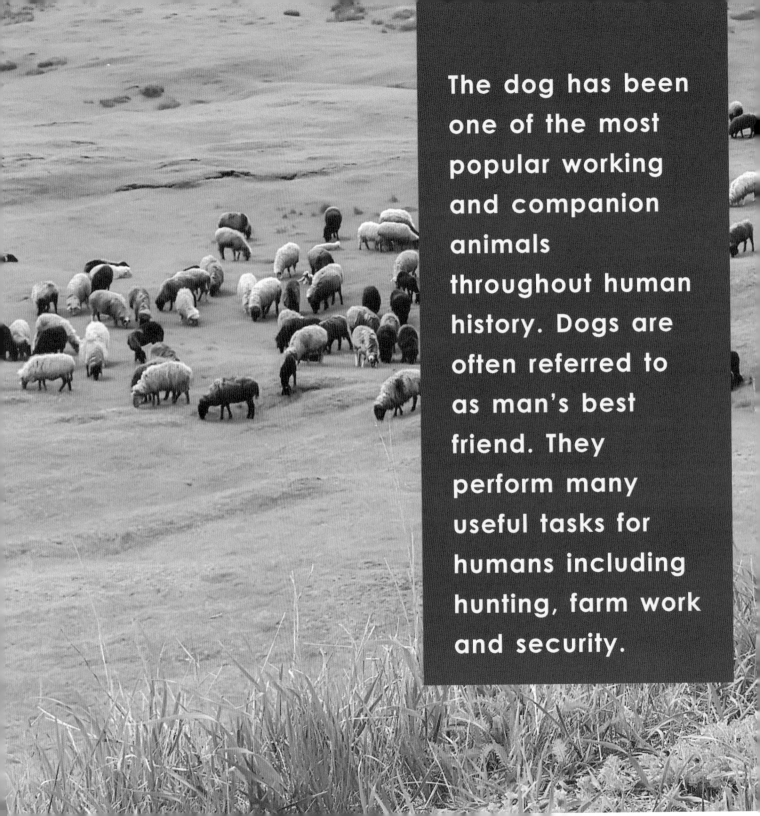

The dog has been one of the most popular working and companion animals throughout human history. Dogs are often referred to as man's best friend. They perform many useful tasks for humans including hunting, farm work and security.

Ducks are mostly aquatic birds living in both fresh water and sea water. Ducks are farmed for their meat, eggs, and down. All ducks have highly waterproof feathers due to the feathers interlocking nature and waxy coating.

Sheep were once wild animals, but were tamed thousands of years ago by humans for their wool, meat, hides and fat. Sheep grow thick fur called wool that grows continuously. Wool has been used for clothing and other fabrics.

Chickens are one of the most common and widespread domestic animals. Chickens are raised mostly for their eggs and meat. The life span of a chicken is about 10 to 15 years.

Made in the USA
Lexington, KY
11 July 2017